FIRST FI[ELD GUIDE TO]
MAMMALS
OF SOUTHERN AFRICA

Lions (page 21)

Gemsbok (page 48)

SEAN FRASER

Contents

Mammals	4
Southern African mammals	5
Identifying mammals	6
Mammal names	7
In the field	8

Scrub Hare (page 14)

Egyptian Slit-faced Bat *Nycteris thebaica*	10
Southern Lesser Galago (Bushbaby) *Galago moholi*	11
Chacma Baboon *Papio ursinus*	12
Vervet Monkey *Cercopithecus pygerythrus*	13
Scrub Hare *Lepus saxatilis*	14
Cape Porcupine *Hystrix africaeaustralis*	15
Cape Ground Squirrel *Xerus inauris*	16
Brown Hyaena *Hyaena brunnea*	17
Spotted Hyaena *Crocuta crocuta*	18
Cheetah *Acinonyx jubatus*	19
Leopard *Panthera pardus*	20
Lion *Panthera leo*	21
Caracal *Caracal caracal*	22
African Wild Cat *Felis silvestris lybica*	23
Bat-eared Fox *Otocyon megalotis*	24
African Wild Dog *Lycaon pictus*	25
Black-backed Jackal *Canis mesomelas*	26
Cape Clawless Otter *Aonyx capensis*	27
Honey Badger *Mellivora capensis*	28
African Civet *Civettictis civetta*	29
Small-spotted Genet *Genetta genetta*	30
Suricate (Meerkat) *Suricata suricatta*	31

Springbok (page 44)

Dwarf Mongoose *Helogale parvula*	32
African Elephant *Loxodonta africana*	33
Rock Hyrax (Dassie) *Procavia capensis*	34
Square-lipped (White) Rhinoceros *Ceratotherium simum*	35
Hook-lipped (Black) Rhinoceros *Diceros bicornis*	36
Plains Zebra *Equus quagga*	37
Warthog *Phacochoerus africanus*	38
Hippopotamus *Hippopotamus amphibius*	39
Giraffe *Giraffa camelopardalis*	40
Blue Wildebeest *Connochaetes taurinus*	41
Blesbok *Damaliscus pygargus phillipsi*	42
Common Duiker *Sylvicapra grimmia*	43
Springbok *Antidorcas marsupialis*	44
Klipspringer *Oreotragus oreotragus*	45
Steenbok *Raphicerus campestris*	46
Impala *Aepyceros melampus*	47
Gemsbok (Oryx) *Oryx gazella*	48
African Buffalo *Syncerus caffer*	49
Kudu *Tragelaphus strepsiceros*	50
Eland *Tragelaphus oryx*	51
Waterbuck *Kobus ellipsiprymnus*	52
Common Dolphin *Delphinus* genus	53
Southern Right Whale *Eubalaena australis*	54
Cape Fur Seal *Arctocephalus pusillus*	55
Glossary	56
Checklist and index	57

Mammals

Mammals are animals with a coat of hair or fur, which keeps their bodies warm. Unlike birds and reptiles, which hatch from eggs, young mammals develop inside their mothers' bodies and are almost fully developed when they are born. After birth they drink milk from their mothers' teats or breasts, until they are able to survive on their own.

Because different mammals live in different environments across the world, and have different habits, their bodies are adapted to the conditions in which they live. Whales have thick layers of fat, called blubber, to keep them warm in cold water; leopards and cheetahs have spots to camouflage them in the long grass when they hunt for prey; and dassies have special pads on their toes to enable them to grip rock surfaces when they climb. Some mammals, such as bats, even have wings so that they can catch their insect prey while they fly.

Gemsbok (page 48)

Southern African mammals

Mammals are found on all the continents of the world. Southern Africa has many different mammal species, ranging from the enormous elephant, the biggest land mammal in the world, to the tiny, mouse-like shrew (not featured in this book) – the world's smallest mammal.

Conservation

Because there is such a variety of fascinating mammals in southern Africa, it is important that we help to protect them. Some southern African mammals, such as the zebra-like quagga (*Equus quagga*), are already extinct; others, like the hook-lipped (black) rhino (*Diceros bicornis*), are endangered, or threatened, and the species could die out entirely if we don't protect it. For this reason, many scientists and researchers study mammals so that we can learn more about them, and through studying them discover how special they are and how we can save them from disappearing altogether.

Cape Fur Seals (page 55)

Cape Ground Squirrel (page 16)

Identifying mammals

Plains Zebra (page 37)

In order to identify a specific mammal, you should study its different features, for example, its **size**, **colour**, and **shape**; also, try to see what **food** it eats, and its surroundings, or **location**. These features may tell you something about the way this mammal lives, and so give you some idea as to what species it is. Different animals have different **habits**, and those with which you may not be familiar are marked with a^G in this book. A definition of these words is given on page 56.

Teach yourself

You can learn about mammals and other animals on your own by teaching yourself:

- Join your local library.
- Use your school library.
- Read magazines on wildlife.
- Read stories about animals.
- Watch television documentary programmes about wildlife.
- Visit zoos, game reserves and parks.
- Visit exhibitions at a natural history museum.
- Ask your teacher.
- Make your own scrapbook.
- Explore the Internet.
- Become a member of a conservation organisation or nature group.
- Go to special talks and lectures at a local university or college.

Mammal names

Most animals are known by a number of different names. They usually have a **common name**, which is familiar to most of us. But because the same, or similar, animals may have different names in different languages all over the world, most scientists, researchers and conservationists prefer to use the animal's **scientific name**. This is usually a Latin name, and is written in italics. The honey badger, for example, is known by scientists as *Mellivora capensis*.

Sometimes animals are also given different common names by the people of a specific region. South African mammals are known by their Afrikaans **(A)**, Xhosa **(X)** or Zulu **(Z)** names, the most commonly spoken languages after English. For example, the honey badger is also known by its Afrikaans name, 'ratel', and/or its Zulu name, 'insele'.

Impala (page 47)

In the field

Leopard (page 20)

Most of the mammals that we discuss in this book are only found in the wild, or in game reserves and national parks. But many, for example squirrels, dassies, bats and even whales, can be observed in the areas where we live or in the surrounding environment.

Where do I go?
- national parks
- game and nature reserves
- zoos
- beaches (whale watching)
- country areas
- conservation groups
- city walks
- your own garden ...

Game viewing
There is a big difference between seeing an animal behind bars in a zoo, and seeing it in its natural environment out in the veld. If you are lucky enough to be able to go game viewing in one of the country's game reserves, take the time to observe not only the animal you are watching, but also everything around it:

the birds, plants, landscape, and sky – otherwise you may just as well visit the zoo.

In the Kruger National Park, it is best to go game viewing in the dry winter months when most animals visit the watering holes to drink. You will, however, see lots of young mammals there in the summer months. In the Kalahari, game viewing is best just after the summer rains. If possible, go out into the bush in the morning and late afternoon only, because when it is hot, most animals rest and hide in the shade. They usually only come out to drink and hunt when it is cooler, and it is during these times that you will be able to observe their habits, and see them eating, grooming one another, marking their territory, fighting, and even playing.

What to take
- binoculars
- camera or video recorder
- notebook and pen
- insect spray
- sun hat and sunscreen
- walking shoes or hiking boots
- field guides and other books

... but, most importantly, be quiet and keep still ...

Chacma Baboon (page 12)

Egyptian Slit-faced Bat

Nycteris thebaica

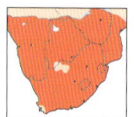

African names: Egiptiese Spleetneusvlermuis (A); Ilulwane (Z).

Average size: Length 10cm; wingspan 25cm; weight 11g.

Identification: Small; dark, woolly hair covers sturdy body. Long, narrow 'slit' runs down the centre of the face, from forehead to nostrils. Ears almost as big as body. Wide wings, rounded at the ends.

Where found: Lives in almost any environment in southern Africa.

Habits: Gregarious[G]; hundreds of bats may roost together in caves, shelters or hollow trees. Nocturnal[G].

Notes: Because bats cannot see very well, the slit in the face has a nose-like function, which enables them to track down prey by using echoes (known as 'echolocation').

Status: Common.

Food: Mostly insects, such as grasshoppers, beetles and moths.

Reproduction: Four-month gestation[G]; single offspring weighing 2g.

Similar species: All other slit-faced bats.

Southern Lesser Galago (Bushbaby)

Galago moholi

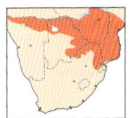

African names: Nagapie (A); Isinkwe (Z).

Average size: Length 35cm; weight 150g.

Identification: The body is small and covered with a velvety coat. The eyes and ears are big and round. The feet are specially adapted for gripping branches, and the bushy tail is used for balance.

Where found: Savanna woodland, fringes of forests, along rivers, in trees that produce gum.

Habits: Feeds mostly on its own, but sleeps in family groups in nest-like structures made of leaves. Arboreal[G], feeding mostly up in trees; territorial[G]. Nocturnal[G].

Notes: Produces a variety of chattering sounds. Some calls resemble a human baby crying.

Status: Common.

Food: Tree gum and resin (especially acacia); also berries, insects and birds' eggs. It derives necessary water requirements from food.

Reproduction: Four-month gestation[G]; one or two young weighing 9g each.

Similar species: Thick-tailed Bushbaby; Grant's Bushbaby.

Chacma Baboon

Papio ursinus

African names: Bobbejaan (A); Imfene (X, Z).

Average size: Length 140cm (m), 110cm (f); weight 32kg (m), 15kg (f).

Identification: Body is relatively large; covered with grey to grey-brown hair. Long, pointed snout. First part of tail is held erect, but the rest hangs straight down. The male has powerful shoulders, with a mane around the neck, and a single patch of bare skin located under the tail. The female has one patch on each buttock.

Where found: Throughout the region in almost any environment, except in very dry parts.

Habits: Terrestrial^G, but also an excellent climber. Highly gregarious^G; troops^G of 15, or even 100, led by a dominant male. Diurnal^G.

Notes: May try to scavenge^G from cars. Never feed baboons.

Status: Common.

Food: Omnivorous^G, but mostly fruit, leaves, seeds, grass, roots.

Reproduction: Six-month gestation^G; single young weighing 800g.

Similar species: Yellow Baboon.

Vervet Monkey

Cercopithecus pygerythrus

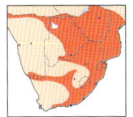

African names: Blou-aap (A); Inkawu (X, Z).

Average size: Length 110cm (m), 100cm (f); weight 6kg (m), 4kg (f).

Identification: Body covered in long, bristly, grey hair; belly is usually much lighter. Single white band stretches across forehead and down sides of cheeks.

Where found: Very adaptable, but generally prefers riverine vegetation in wooded areas and rocky terrain.

Habits: Gregarious[G]; troops[G] of up to 20. Good climber, but usually forages on the ground. Diurnal[G].

Notes: Noisy; produces loud chattering and scream-like noises and a distinctive alarm bark to warn troop[G] when a predator is spotted.

Status: Common.

Food: Mainly fruit, flowers, leaves and insects.

Reproduction: Five-month gestation[G]; single young weighing 350g.

Scrub Hare

Lepus saxatilis

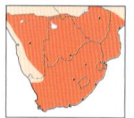

African names: Kolhaas (A); Umvundla (X); Unogwaja (Z).

Average size: Length 60cm; weight 3kg.

Identification: Most noted for its very long ears and powerful hindlegs. Coat is soft and fluffy, and dark grey in colour. Tail is small and fuzzy.

Where found: Savanna, woodland and grassland with long grass, bushes and shrubs.

Habits: Usually lives on its own. Nocturnal[G]; rests in small hollows in the ground during the day. Moves about by hopping.

Notes: Strong back legs make hares good jumpers and runners.

The white undertail is very noticeable when it is on the move. Zimbabwe specimens are smaller.

Status: Common.

Food: Grazes[G] on grass, leaves and grass roots. Sometimes browses[G] on low bushes.

Reproduction: One to three leverets (young hares) weighing 250g each are born after a one-and-a-half-month gestation[G] period.

Similar species: Cape Hare.

Cape Porcupine

Hystrix africaeaustralis

African names: Ystervark (A); Incanda (X); Ingungumbane (Z).

Average size: Length 90cm; height 35cm; weight 18kg.

Identification: Heavily built creature with a coat of long black-and-white quills extending from the shoulders to the tail. The short, flat tail is covered with white spines. Ridge of softer spines on blunt, rounded head.

Where found: It has very few specific habitat requirements and is therefore found virtually anywhere in the region; usually in burrows^G, caves or crevices in rocks.

Habits: Lives in extended family group with only one breeding pair in each group. Nocturnal^G; sleeps in holes. Forages along set paths and burrows^G.

Notes: When threatened, it rattles and shakes its quills to scare off enemies; attacks by running backwards (and slightly sideways) to stab attacker with sharp quills.

Status: Common.

Food: Mostly plant matter.

Reproduction: Three-month gestation^G; one or two young weighing 200g each.

Similar species: Hedgehog.

Cape Ground Squirrel

Xerus inauris

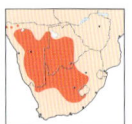

African names: Waaierstert-grondeekhoring (A); Unomatse, wasemhlabeni (X); Ingwejeje yaphansi (Z).

Average size: Length 55cm; weight 750g.

Identification: Small, with short, prickly body hair. Usually greyish-brown in colour with a fainter stripe down each side of the body. Small, pointed face with tiny ears. Long, fluffy tail with black-and-white markings.

Where found: Dry, open areas with little vegetation.

Habits: Highly gregarious[G]; large groups of between four and 30 with several dominant females. Diurnal[G]; may use its bushy tail to shade body from sun. Digs very long burrows[G] in which it sleeps. Terrestrial[G].

Notes: Always on the lookout for predators; gives a loud whistle when it senses danger.

Status: Common.

Food: Mostly vegetarian. Diet includes roots, bulbs, grass, pods and seeds.

Reproduction: One-and-a-half-month gestation[G]; two or three young weighing 20g each.

Similar species: Yellow Mongoose.

Brown Hyaena

Hyaena brunnea

African names: Strandwolf, Bruin Hiëna (A); Ingqawane, Ingcuka (X); Isidawana (Z).

Average size: Length 150cm; height 80cm; weight 45kg.

Identification: High shoulders, sloping back, low rump, all covered with a shaggy, dark brown coat; the mane-like patch of hair around the neck is lighter. Big head with sharply pointed ears. Striped legs.

Where found: Prefers dry areas such as the Kalahari and Namib Desert in Namibia.

Habits: Moves around on its own, but shares territory with as many as 10 others. Marks territories with droppings and secretions from anal glands. Nocturnal[G].

Notes: Often stores extra food in special 'pantries'.

Status: Near threatened.

Food: Mainly scavenges[G], but may also eat small creatures and even fruit.

Reproduction: Three-month gestation[G]; litter[G] of two or four cubs weighing 420g each.

Similar species: Spotted Hyaena.

Spotted Hyaena

Crocuta crocuta

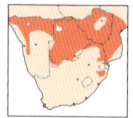

African names: Gevlekte Hiëna (A); Ingcuka-cheya (X).

Average size: Length 150cm; height 80cm; weight 70kg.

Identification: High shoulders, sloping back, low rump; yellow-brown coat covered with dark splotches; mane-like patch of hair around neck. Big head with large, rounded ears. Short, hairy tail.

Where found: Open plains, woodland savanna and dry areas.

Habits: Usually lives in family groups known as clans, in which females are dominant. Territorial[G]. Marks territories with droppings and secretions from anal glands. Nocturnal[G]. Expert hunter.

Notes: Known as the 'laughing' hyaena; makes human-like chuckling sounds; also shrieks and growls. Its oud 'whoop' call is characteristic of the African night.

Status: Common in protected areas only.

Food: Hunts antelope and zebra but may also scavenge[G].

Reproduction: Three-and-a-half-month gestation[G]; litter[G] of one to two cubs weighing 1.5kg each.

Similar species: Brown Hyaena.

Cheetah

Acinonyx jubatus

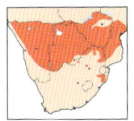

African names: Jagluiperd (A); Ingwenkala (X); Ingulule (Z).

Average size: Length 2m; height 1m; weight 50kg.

Identification: The lean body and long legs are pale and covered with black spots from the tail to the head. Black stripes, or 'tears', run down the sides of the face, from the inner eye to the outer corner of the mouth.

Where found: Open spaces and areas with only a few trees.

Habits: Females live alone with their cubs. Males live alone or in groups of two or three. Hunts during the cooler times of the day by stalking victim and then making a quick dash for the kill.

Notes: Fastest land animal in the world, reaching about 100km/h over short distances.

Status: Vulnerable.

Food: Feeds on birds, and small and medium-sized antelope.

Reproduction: Three-month gestation[G]; litter[G] of three cubs weighing 300g each.

Similar species: Leopard.

Leopard

Panthera pardus

African names: Luiperd (A); Ihlosi (X); Ingwe (Z).

Average size: Length 190cm; height 80cm; weight 80kg (m), 50kg (f).

Identification: Big and strong; powerful jaws. Body is light-coloured and covered with small rosettes^G. Legs, head and rump are covered with black spots; belly is white. Long, rosette^G-covered tail is white underneath.

Where found: Able to live in almost any environment.

Habits: Solitary and territorial^G; marks territory with droppings and urine. Nocturnal^G. Hunts by stalking, and then leaping out onto prey.

Notes: Well camouflaged in trees and tall grasses.

Status: Near threatened.

Food: Feeds on birds, antelope, dassies – and even rats and mice.

Reproduction: Three-and-a-half-month gestation^G; one to three cubs weighing 500g each.

Similar species: Cheetah.

Lion

Panthera leo

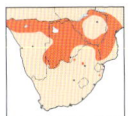

African names: Leeu (A); Ingonyama (X); Ibhubesi (Z).

Average size: Length 3m (m), 2.5m (f); height 1.5m (m), 1.2m (f); weight 200kg (m), 140kg (f).

Identification: Largest African predator; light brown to brownish-red in colour; long tail is short-haired and ends in a dark tuft of hair. Male has a long, bushy mane around the head and throat.

Where found: Able to live in almost any habitat.

Habits: Lives in prides^G of usually two or three males, and several females and their offspring. Females hunt together in groups.

Notes: Lionesses are responsible for the hunting, usually at night or towards nightfall. Hunt by ambushing prey; males eat first.

Status: Vulnerable.

Food: Hunts most large mammals, including antelope.

Reproduction: Three-and-a-half-month gestation^G; one to four cubs weighing 1.5kg each.

Caracal

Caracal caracal

African names: Rooikat (A); Ingqawa (X); Indabushe (Z).

Average size: Length 50cm; height 90cm; weight 12kg.

Identification: Body covered with soft, red-coloured hair. High rump; short tail. Very sharp, black-backed ears with silvery-grey hairs on the inside and a tuft of black hair on each tip. White chin, with white lines under the eyes and nose.

Where found: Able to survive in almost any habitat, except for coastal areas.

Habits: Lives on its own. Nocturnal[G], but may be active during the day.

Notes: Because it has been known to attack farm animals such as sheep and goats, the caracal is one of the most hunted mammals in southern Africa.

Status: Common.

Food: Rodents, reptiles, ground-nesting birds, and small mammals such as dassies; may even kill impala and bushbuck lambs.

Reproduction: Two-and-a-half-month gestation[G]; two or three kittens weighing 250g each.

African Wild Cat

Felis silvestris lybica

African names: Vaalboskat (A); Imbodla (X, Z); Ingada, Ichathaza (X); Impaka (Z).

Average size: Length 90cm; height 40cm; weight 4kg.

Identification: Body colour depends on the wild cat's habitat, but is usually light brown to grey. The throat and the area under the mouth are usually white in colour, and the underparts, the ears and the back legs are red.

Where found: Prefers to live in areas that are sheltered with long grass and a few trees and bushes.

Habits: Usually lives alone. Territorial^G; marks its territories with urine. Hunts in similar manner to domestic cat.

Notes: Able to crossbreed with tame, household cats.

Status: Common.

Food: Feeds mostly on rabbits, mice, rats, snakes and birds, as well as insects and occasionally even spiders.

Reproduction: After a two-month gestation^G period, three or four kittens, weighing 45g each, are born.

Similar species: Small-spotted Cat.

Bat-eared Fox

Otocyon megalotis

African names: Bakoorjakkals (A); Impungushe enamadlebe elulwane (Z).

Average size: Length 90cm; height 30cm; weight 4kg.

Identification: Small, silvery-grey body and black legs. Ears are disproportionately big, compared to small, sharply pointed face; has a grey-white patch over the eyes and nose.

Where found: Occurs fairly commonly in the region, mostly in open scrub grassland.

Habits: Usually lives in pairs or in tight family groups. Mostly nocturnal[G]. Digs burrows[G] and holes to find food.

Notes: Not a true fox.

Status: Common.

Food: Insects such as harvester termites, and also berries and sometimes small vertebrates.

Reproduction: Two-and-a-half-month gestation[G]; litter[G] of one to five pups usually weighing about 400g each.

Similar species: Cape Fox.

African Wild Dog

Lycaon pictus

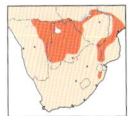

African names: Wildehond (A); Ixhwili (X); Inja yasendle (Z).

Average size: Length 130cm; height 80cm; weight 25kg.

Identification: Patches of yellow, white, black and brown hair cover the thin body and long, slender legs. Face is pale, but mouth area is dark; dark stripe runs between eyes to top of head. Ears are dark and round. Tufted tail is mostly white.

Where found: Savanna woodlands and hilly country; also open plains and areas with short grass and little vegetation.

Habits: Live in packs of about 12; hunt together during early morning or late afternoon. Relentlessly pursue prey; seldom give up until they have made a kill. They only kill to eat. There is only one breeding pair per pack.

Notes: One of Africa's most endangered mammals.

Status: Endangered.

Food: Impala and small antelope.

Reproduction: A two-and-a-half-month gestation[G] period after which a litter[G] of seven to 12 pups weighing 300g each are born.

Black-backed Jackal

Canis mesomelas

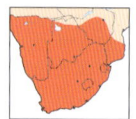

African names: Rooijakkals (A); Impungushe emhlane omnyama (Z).

Average size: Length 100cm; height 45cm; weight 8kg.

Identification: Reddish in colour with broad stripe of silvery-black along back, and black tail. Sharp, pointed ears with tufts of white hair inside. Areas around the lower mouth, under the neck and on the chest are almost white.

Where found: Usually prefers dry areas, but is found almost throughout the region.

Habits: Usually lives alone, in pairs or in small family packs. Nocturnal[G].

Notes: Known to be very clever, and constantly on the lookout for danger. Wails towards nightfall; also yaps.

Status: Common.

Food: Feeds on mice, birds, snakes, lizards and fruit, and even small buck. Also carrion[G].

Reproduction: Two-month gestation[G]; litter[G] of one to six pups weighing 380g each.

Similar species: Side-striped Jackal.

Cape Clawless Otter

Aonyx capensis

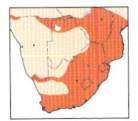

African names: Groototter (A); Intini (X); Umthini waseKapa ongenazindlawu (Z).

Average size: Length 140cm; weight 14kg.

Identification: Long, sleek body with dark coat; white throat and chest. Thick, sturdy legs and strong tail. Finger-like toes rather than obvious claws.

Where found: Found in vegetation along freshwater habitats, as well as in marine areas.

Habits: Lives alone, or female with young. Active at almost any time. Uses fingers to sift through water and silt for food.

Notes: Uses powerful tail and slightly webbed toes to propel body through water; head is often above the surface. Rough patches under fingers help it to hold onto slippery prey.

Status: Widespread, but not common.

Food: Mostly freshwater crabs and mussels, also frogs and fish.

Reproduction: Two-month gestation[G]; litter[G] of two or three cubs weighing 250g each.

Similar species: Spotted-necked Otter; Water Mongoose.

Honey Badger

Mellivora capensis

African names: Ratel (A); Ichelesi (X); Insele (Z).

Average size: Length 95cm; height 35cm; weight 11kg.

Identification: Thickset body. Broad, silvery grey stripe along the back. Legs are short and tail is short and bushy. Powerful, sharp front claws. Strong jaws and teeth.

Where found: Throughout southern Africa, except in desert regions and areas with thick vegetation.

Habits: Mainly lives alone. Nocturnal[G]. Aggressive fighter. Smelly odour released from anal glands when stressed.

Notes: Honeyguide bird said to lead badger to beehives.

Status: Common, but protected locally.

Food: Insects, beetle larvae, reptiles, rodents, and birds' eggs.

Reproduction: Six-month gestation[G]; two or three young weighing 300g each.

African Civet

Civettictis civetta

African names: Siwet (A); Inyhwagi (X); Iqaqa (Z).

Average size: Length 130cm; height 45cm; weight 12kg.

Identification: Body covered with long, greyish hair and dark splotches and stripes. Grey face, with black bands across eyes and white muzzle; throat covered with black-and-white bands. Legs are long; dark stripe runs down bushy tail.

Where found: Usually lives in areas with good vegetation and a regular supply of water.

Habits: Lives on its own. Nocturnal[G]. Marks territory with secretions from anal glands.

Notes: Usually arches its back while walking. Mane-like ridge of coarse hair becomes erect when it senses danger.

Status: Locally common.

Food: Feeds on carrion[G], but prefers millipedes, insects, rodents, reptiles, small birds and wild fruits.

Reproduction: Two-month gestation[G]; litter[G] of one to four cubs weighing 100g each.

Similar species: Tree Civet, Small-spotted Genet.

Small-spotted Genet

Genetta genetta

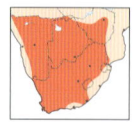

African names: Kleinkolmuskeljaatkat (A); Inyhwagi (X); Insimba enamachashaza (Z).

Average size: Length 90cm; height 25cm; weight 2.5kg.

Identification: The body is usually a pale, whitish colour with a grey tint, and is covered with small, dark-coloured spots and blotches. There are white patches around the eyes, the muzzle is dark, and the ears are big and almost transparent. The tail is long and ringed with wide black bands.

Where found: Able to live almost anywhere in southern Africa.

Habits: Normally solitary. Nocturnal^G, but sometimes seen during the day. Terrestrial^G, but a good climber.

Notes: Musky odour released from scent glands when stressed.

Status: Common.

Food: Feeds mostly on insects, but also takes rats, mice, birds, snakes, lizards, frogs, scorpions and fruit.

Reproduction: Two-and-a-half-month gestation^G; three or four young weighing 65g each.

Similar species: African Civet; Large-spotted Genet.

Suricate (Meerkat)

Suricata suricatta

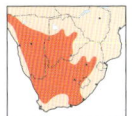

African names: Stokstertmeerkat (A); Igala (X); Ububhibhi (Z).

Average size: Length 50cm; height 20cm; weight 800g.

Identification: Sharply pointed face, with dark patches around the eyes. Small, lean body of either light brown or light grey; thin tail.

Where found: Dry, open areas.

Habits: Extremely gregarious^G; occurring in groups of between five and 40. Diurnal^G.

Notes: The thin, strong tail is held upright when the suricate runs, but is used for balance when the animal stands up on its back legs.

Status: Locally common.

Food: Mostly insects, but also snakes and lizards.

Reproduction: Two-and-a-half-month gestation^G; three or four young weighing 50g each.

Similar species: Banded Mongoose.

Dwarf Mongoose

Helogale parvula

African name: Dwergmuishond (A).

Average size: Length 35cm; height 15cm; weight 300g.

Identification: Small, thin body covered with a red-brown, short-haired coat; long, hairy tail. Pointed face, with small, rounded ears.

Where found: Open woodlands. Favours termite mounds for dens, but will utilise hollow trees or even deep crevices in rocks.

Habits: Live together in packs, with a dominant breeding pair. All pack members help to raise the young.

Notes: Smallest mongoose. Its tail is as long as its body.

Status: Common.

Food: Mostly insects and small invertebrates, and sometimes birds and lizards.

Reproduction: Two-month gestation[G]; litter[G] of one to seven young weighing about 20g each.

Similar species: Banded Mongoose.

African Elephant

Loxodonta africana

African names: Olifant (A); Indlovu (X, Z).

Average size: Height 3.4m (m), 2.5m (f); weight 6,000kg (m), 3,500kg (f).

Identification: World's largest land mammal, grey-brown in colour, with a thick, leathery skin. Trunk 1.5m long; big ears, tusks.

Where found: Dry savanna and woodland. Needs plenty of food and water.

Habits: Small family groups of mothers and calves led by an old cow. Bulls live separately in small groups.

Notes: Usually not dangerous, but will charge if wounded or when protecting calves.

Status: Vulnerable.

Food: Eats about 300kg of plants, fruits, leaves and grass, and drinks about 200 litres of water in a day.

Reproduction: 22-month gestation[G]; single calf weighing 120kg. Only breed every three to four years.

Rock Hyrax (Dassie)

Procavia capensis

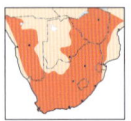

African names: Klipdassie (A); Imbila (X, Z).

Average size: Length 50cm; height 30cm; weight 3.5kg.

Identification: Small, stocky body covered with light to dark brown hair; no tail. Sharply pointed face; small, rounded ears. Short legs; glands on feet secrete moisture which enables animal to grip rock surfaces.

Where found: Rocky, mountainous terrain.

Habits: Lives in groups of up to 17 females together with their young, with a single dominant male. Diurnal[G], but may feed at night.

Notes: One adult keeps guard while others feed or lie in the sun; gives a warning call when sees or hears danger, so that group can take cover (usually nearby).

Status: Common.

Food: Leaves, fruit and grass.

Reproduction: Seven-month gestation[G]; two or three young weighing 200g each.

Similar species: Tree Dassie, Yellow-spotted Rock Dassie.

Square-lipped (White) Rhinoceros

Ceratotherium simum

Vulnerable to poaching: population distribution confidential.

African names: Witrenoster (A); Umkhombe omhlope (X); Ubhejane omhlophe (Z).

Average size: Height 1.8m; weight 1,800kg.

Identification: Lips are square-shaped. Has two horns, and big, pointed ears. Prominent hump on the back of the neck.

Where found: Lots of short grass, shady bushes and fresh water.

Habits: Lives in groups of three or four; males territorial[G]. Poor eyesight, but quick to respond to dangerous sounds or smells.

Notes: Because it regularly rolls in the dust, it appears sand-coloured. A rhino's horns are made of a hair-like fibre, not of bone or ivory.

Status: Near threatened.

Food: Grazer[G]; feeds on short grasses and low-growing plants.

Reproduction: 16-month gestation[G]; single calf weighing 40kg.

Similar species: Hook-lipped (Black) Rhinoceros.

Hook-lipped (Black) Rhinoceros

Diceros bicornis

Critically endangered: population distribution confidential.

African names: Swartrenoster (A); Umkhombe omnyama (X); Ubhejane omnyama (Z).

Average size: Height 1.5m; weight 900kg.

Identification: Greyish-brown in colour with thick skin. Two horns and short tail. Pointed upper lip hooks over the bottom lip. Head is smaller than white rhino's.

Where found: From deserts to areas with shrubs and trees that give plenty of shade.

Habits: Lives alone. Poor eyesight, but possesses a keen sense of smell.

Notes: Drops its dung in special areas called middens^G or latrines^G. Searches for food when it is cool.

Status: Critically endangered.

Food: Browser^G. Uses its pointed upper lip to pull leaves and twigs from shrubs.

Reproduction: 15-month gestation^G; single calf weighing 40kg.

Similar species: Square-lipped (White) Rhinoceros.

Plains Zebra

Equus quagga

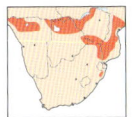

African names: Vlaktesebra (A); Iqwarha (X); Idube lasethafeni (Z).

Average Size: Height 1.3m; weight 300kg.

Identification: Black-and-white striped coat; shadow stripes are superimposed on white stripes. Long mane of black-and-white hair extends from top of head to shoulders.

Where found: Areas of open grassland and woodland.

Habits: Lives in small family groups, but may also be seen grazing^G with antelope, such as wildebeest.

Notes: Young males may form bachelor^G herds. Stallions are fiercely protective of their mares.

Status: Common in protected areas.

Food: Grazes^G on grasses, but may also browse^G on leaves and shoots.

Reproduction: 12-month gestation^G; single foal weighing 30kg.

Similar species: Cape Mountain Zebra.

Warthog

Phacochoerus africanus

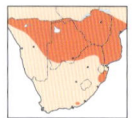

African names: Vlakvark (A); Inxagu (X); Intibane (Z).

Average size: Height 70cm (m), 60cm (f); weight 80kg (m), 60kg (f).

Identification: Powerful body and a pig-like face with a long snout. Pronounced bumps ('warts') located above the nostrils and on either side of the eyes. Grey skin covered with scattered bristly hair. Long-haired mane and a very thin tail, ending in a clump of hair. Adults have curved tusks, and whisker-like hairs on the sides of the face.

Where found: Prefers wide, open woodlands.

Habits: Family groups (called 'sounders') consist of a mother and her litter[G]; these sometimes include a boar, although boars are usually found in bachelor[G] herds. Diurnal[G].

Notes: Tail is held upright when running. Kneels on its front legs when feeding. Uses its tusks (two pairs) as weapons – these are actually canine teeth.

Status: Common.

Food: Mostly grazers[G], feeding on grass and plant roots.

Reproduction: Six-month gestation[G]; two or three piglets weighing 600g each.

Similar species: Bushpig.

Hippopotamus

Hippopotamus amphibius

African names: Seekoei (A); Imvubu (X, Z).

Average size: Height 1.5m; weight 1,500kg.

Identification: Huge body covered in smooth, dark grey skin. Massive, powerful jaws; huge canine and incisor teeth. Short legs, with four toes on each foot.

Where found: Rivers, lakes and lagoons.

Habits: Lives in groups of about 12 cows and calves, headed by a bull. Roams river banks at night. Bulls mark their territory by spreading their dung.

Notes: Can hold breath under water for five or six minutes. Nostrils close automatically when the head is underwater. Body produces red-coloured liquid to keep skin moist.

Status: Vulnerable.

Food: Grazer[G]; feeds mostly on grass and small plants that are found on or near river banks and lagoons.

Reproduction: Mates in the water; eight-month gestation[G]; single calf weighing 30kg.

Giraffe

Giraffa camelopardalis

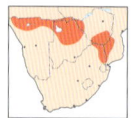

African names: Kameelperd (A); Indlulamthi (X); Indlulamithi (Z).

Average size: Height 4.5m (m), 4m (f); weight 1,200kg (m), 900kg (f).

Identification: Tall; long, thin legs and long, sturdy neck. Coat covered with mottled brown patches. Sharp, pointed face; two horn-like knobs (covered with skin) on the head.

Where found: Thornveld.

Habits: Lives in groups of up to 20; most active in early morning and late afternoon.

Notes: Makes snorting sounds. It is the tallest land mammal.

Status: Locally common.

Food: Browser[G]; spends three-quarters of day eating from high branches. Curls its lips and 45cm tongue around twigs and pulls off leaves. Favours acacia trees.

Reproduction: 15-month gestation[G]; single calf weighing 100kg.

Blue Wildebeest

Connochaetes taurinus

African names: Blouwildebees (A); Inkonkoni eluhlaza okwesi bhakabhaka (Z).

Average size: Height 1.5m (m), 1.3m (f); weight 250kg (m), 180kg (f).

Identification: Dark grey body, broad chest and wide shoulders. Stripe-like marks run from neck to chest. Broad face with hair hanging from the throat; pair of curved horns; long-haired tail.

Where found: Open savanna and grassy plains.

Habits: Gregarious[G]. Usually herds of up to 30, but sometimes thousands when migrating[G]. Bulls are strictly territorial[G].

Notes: Calves can walk almost immediately after they are born. Its horns are not as curved as black wildebeest's.

Status: Common.

Food: Grazes[G] on short grasses.

Reproduction: Eight-month gestation[G]; single calf weighing 20kg.

Similar species: Black Wildebeest.

Blesbok

Damaliscus pygargus phillipsi

African names: Blesbok (A); Iling'a (X); Indluzele empemvu (Z).

Average size: Height 90cm; weight 70kg.

Identification: Strong chest and low rump covered with a short-haired coat of red-brown; saddle and underparts lighter. Long, white muzzle, and pointed white ears. Both sexes have ridged horns that curve outwards.

Where found: Prefers wide, open spaces and grassy plains.

Habits: Form herds; bulls are strictly territorial[G]. , They flee in a long line, when frightened. Create their own middens[G].

Notes: Both males and females have horns.

Status: Common.

Food: Exclusively a grazer[G].

Reproduction: Eight-month gestation[G]; single lamb weighing 6kg.

Similar species: Bontebok.

Common Duiker

Sylvicapra grimmia

African names: Gewone Duiker (A); Impunzi eqhelekileyo (X); Impunzi (Z).

Average size: Height 60cm; weight 18kg.

Identification: Small body with grey to dark brown coat of short hair, and long, thin legs. Tuft of long hair on top of the head; may have a stripe of dark hair on the snout. Rams have sharply pointed horns.

Where found: Commonly found in most areas, but prefers bushy terrain and wooded savanna.

Habits: Usually lives on its own, but also seen in pairs. Territorial^G. Ram holds territory with one, sometimes two, ewes. Diurnal^G in wilderness regions.

Notes: Small glands on inner eyes secrete a substance that is rubbed off on twigs and grass stems to mark territories.

Status: Abundant.

Food: Browses^G on shoots, leaves, flowers, fruit, and even farm crops. Has also been known to eat insects, and even carrion^G.

Reproduction: Six-month gestation^G; single lamb weighing 1.5kg.

Similar species: Blue Duiker, Red Duiker, Oribi, Klipspringer.

Springbok

Antidorcas marsupialis

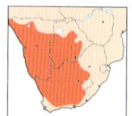

African names: Springbok (A); Ibhadi (X); Insephe (Z).

Average size: Height 75cm; weight 40kg.

Identification: Small body; light brown back, white belly, and broad, dark red-brown stripe on the sides. Thin, strong legs, and long, pointed ears. Both ram and ewe have curved, ridged horns, but the male's horns are thicker. Tiny tail.

Where found: Dry, open areas with little vegetation.

Habits: Usually form small herds, but may come together in thousands, especially during migration[G].

Notes: When frightened, the springbok 'pronks', leaping straight-legged into the air with its back arched.

Status: Common.

Food: Largely a grazer[G], but may also browse[G].

Reproduction: Five-and-a-half-month gestation[G]; single lamb weighing 3.5kg.

Klipspringer

Oreotragus oreotragus

African names: Klipspringer (A); Igogo (X, Z).

Average size: Height 60cm; weight 12kg.

Identification: Fairly small antelope with rough, bristly coat. Body greyish in colour, but belly and lower face almost white. Short, rounded ears, and bead-like eyes. Only male has short, pointed horns.

Where found: Only in very rocky areas.

Habits: Live in pairs with most recent offspring. Active in morning and late afternoon.

Notes: Only antelope that walks on the tips of its small hooves. Special glands located under the eyes give off a secretion that is used to mark territory on twigs and branches.

Status: Common.

Food: Usually browses[G], but sometimes eats grasses.

Reproduction: Seven-month gestation[G]; single lamb weighing 1kg.

Steenbok

Raphicerus campestris

African names: Steenbok (A); Itshabanqa (X); Iqhina (Z).

Average size: Height 50cm; weight 13kg.

Identification: Small, graceful body covered with light brown coat; white on the belly. Small head with white patch on the neck and around the eyes; large ears. Rams have short, sharply pointed horns.

Where found: Usually in open grasslands with some trees and rocks for shelter.

Habits: Usually lives on its own, but a pair share a territory, which they defend. May be active during day and night. Creates its own middens[G], which are lightly covered with soil.

Notes: Runs very fast in zigzag pattern as it flees, and may stop to look back.

Status: Abundant.

Food: Mainly browses[G] on young leaves, shoots, flowers and fruit. May also dig for roots with its hooves.

Reproduction: Six-month gestation[G]; single lamb weighing 900g.

Similar species: Sharpe's Grysbok, Oribi.

Impala

Aepyceros melampus

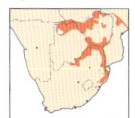

African names: Rooibok (A); Impala (X, Z).

Average size: Height 90cm; weight 50kg.

Identification: Medium-sized, with a red-coloured back, slightly lighter sides, and white underparts. Only rams have the outward-curving horns.

Where found: Open woodland areas with some cover from predators (bushes and small trees).

Habits: Rams live in bachelor[G] herds; females form herds during the mating season. Diurnal[G].

Notes: Has gland above hoof on each hindleg that is used to mark territory.

Status: Common.

Food: Grazer[G].

Reproduction: Seven-and-a-half-month gestation[G]; single lamb weighing 5kg.

Similar species: Black-faced Impala.

Gemsbok (Oryx)

Oryx gazella

African names: Gemsbok (A); I-gemsbok (Z); Inkukhama (X).

Average size: Height 1.2m; weight 220kg.

Identification: Solid body; greyish in colour, with clear black-and-white marks on face, upper legs, rump and lower body. A broad, black stripe runs down the throat. Thick neck. Tail of long, dark hair. Both male and female have long, straight horns.

Where found: Prefers dry grassland and desert dunes.

Habits: Herds are comprised of approximately 15 animals; these consist of bulls, cows and calves, or cows and calves only. Bulls are territorial[G].

Notes: To prevent the gemsbok's brain from overheating, blood passes through a special cooling system in the animal's nose, and once it has cooled down, flows on to the brain.

Status: Locally common.

Food: Eats mainly dry grass or shrubs; also wild melons for their moisture content. Can survive mostly without water.

Reproduction: Nine-month gestation[G]; single calf weighing 15kg.

African Buffalo

Syncerus caffer

African names: Buffel (A); Inyathi (X, Z).

Average size: Height 1.4m; weight 700kg.

Identification: Sturdy, dark brown body and wide, strong back. Short legs and large hooves. Ears are long and hang below the face. Tuft of dark hair on the tip of the tail. Males and females have massive, curved horns.

Where found: Prefers woodland savanna.

Habits: Gregarious[G]; lives in herds, which can include hundreds of animals – males, females and their young. Some bulls may form small bachelor[G] herds.

Notes: Although both cows and bulls have big horns, the bull usually has a much heavier 'boss', or hard, cap-like base of the horn.

Status: Locally common.

Food: Grazer[G].

Reproduction: 11-month gestation[G]; single calf weighing 40kg.

Kudu

Tragelaphus strepsiceros

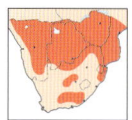

African names: Koedoe (A); Iqhude (X); Umgankla (Z).

Average size: Height 150cm; weight 250kg (m), 180kg (f).

Identification: Light brown to greyish-brown in colour, with six to 10 pale, narrow stripes running vertically along each side of the body. Bulls more grey than cows. Has large, leaf-shaped ears. Bushy, brown tail is white underneath, with a black tip. The bull has impressive spiral horns.

Where found: Lives in savanna woodland areas, as well as dry, rocky patches of land.

Habits: Cows and calves form herds of about four to 10 animals, while bulls live either on their own or in bachelor[G] herds. Diurnal[G].

Notes: Excellent jumpers, kudu can reach heights of over 2m!

Status: Common.

Food: Browser[G]; eats the leaves of an enormous variety of different bushes and low trees – more than any other antelope in southern Africa.

Reproduction: Seven-month gestation[G]; single calf weighing about 15kg.

Eland

Tragelaphus oryx

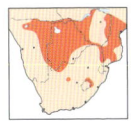

African names: Eland (A); Impofu (X, Z).

Average size: Height 1.7m (m), 1.5m (f); weight 750kg (m), 450kg (f).

Identification: Huge, cow-like body. Dark mane running down the neck; long tail, which ends in a clump of dark hair. Both bull and cow have slightly twisted horns.

Where found: Savanna woodland and dry plains.

Habits: Usually in herds of 20 to 60, but these can sometimes come together for short periods to form large groups of more than 1,000 animals.

Notes: Can survive without drinking water for long periods, instead relying on wild cucumbers and melons for moisture intake.

Status: Locally common.

Food: Browses[G], but also digs for roots. Can go for long periods without water.

Reproduction: Nine-month gestation[G]; single calf weighing about 30kg.

Waterbuck

Kobus ellipsiprymnus

African names: Waterbok (A); Iphiva (X, Z).

Average size: Height 1.2m; weight 220kg.

Identification: Well-built body with shaggy, greyish or brown coat. Males have long, ridged horns that curve upwards. Distinct white ring around the rump area.

Where found: Almost always near water; prefers dense, woody vegetation with tall grass.

Habits: Gregarious[G]. Small herds of about 10, with one adult bull. Young bulls may form bachelor[G] herds.

Notes: Bulls are strictly territorial[G], especially during mating season.

Status: Common.

Food: Grazes[G] predominantly on grasses, but may also browse[G].

Reproduction: Nine-month gestation[G]; single calf weighing 13kg.

Common Dolphin

Delphinus genus

African names: Gewone Dolfyn (A); Ihlengesi eliqhelekileyo (X); Ihlengethwa elivamile (Z).

Average size: Length 2.5m; weight 150kg.

Identification: Dark grey back, with grey and mustard-coloured shapes on the sides; dark stripe from around the eyes down into long beak. Sharp, curved dorsal fin; long, tapered pectoral fins.

Where found: Shallow and deep, warm pelagic (sea) waters throughout the region.

Habits: Commonly found in groups of about 20. Dives underwater for only short periods. Jumps out of the water when chasing flying fish.

Notes: Curved crisscross pattern along its sides.

Food: Small fish, such as anchovies and sardines, and squid.

Reproduction: 11-month gestation^G; single calf is 1m long and weighs 40kg.

Status: Common offshore.

Similar species: Bottlenose Dolphin.

Southern Right Whale

Eubalaena australis

African names: Suidkaper (A); Umnenga (X); Umkhoma (Z).

Average size: Length 17m; weight 60t.

Identification: Very large, dark grey body, with heavy front, tapering towards the large, pointed flukes (at end of tail). Pectoral fins shaped like a paddle; no dorsal fin. Head is very large. Whale lice and barnacles settle on areas of thick skin (callosities) on head – making them white.

Where found: Migrates^G between waters of the Antarctic (November to April) and oceans north and south of the tropics (May to October).

Habits: Occurs in small pods. Swims slowly. Whales 'breach', or push their bodies backwards out of the sea, then crash back down into the water.

Notes: Called southern 'right' whale because was considered by early whalers as the 'right' whale to hunt, because it floats when dead.

Status: Seasonally common.

Food: Specialist feeder on copepods^G.

Reproduction: 12-month gestation^G; single calf weighing 1t.

Cape Fur Seal

Arctocephalus pusillus

African names: Kaapse Pelsrob (A); Imvu yamanzi yaseKape (Z).

Average size: Length 220cm (m), 160cm (f); weight 250kg (m), 75kg (f).

Identification: Torpedo-shaped body covered in dark brown, almost black hair. Males are especially dark, with mane-like hair around the throat and neck. Four flippers. Whiskers on side of pointed face.

Where found: Coastal land and water.

Habits: Live in colonies of hundreds when breeding. Adult bulls mark out territories at breeding spots.

Notes: About seven days after giving birth to her pup, the mother returns to the sea to hunt. On her return, she calls for her pup who recognises her immediately by her call.

Status: Locally common.

Food: Prefers fish that swim in large schools, such as pilchards and sardines.

Reproduction: Gestation[G] approximately 12 months; single offspring weighing 3kg.

Similar species: Other seal species.

Glossary

Arboreal: Living in trees.
Bachelor: Non-breeding male.
Browser: An animal that feeds on the leaves and fruits of trees and bushes.
Burrow: A tunnel or hole dug in the ground to offer shelter.
Carrion: Dead and rotting meat.
Copepods: One of the many micro-organisms that make up plankton.
Diurnal: Active during the day.
Gestation: Pregnancy; time during which developing young is carried in the womb of the mother.
Grazer: An animal that feeds mostly on grass and groundcover plants.
Gregarious: Social; living in groups or colonies.
Latrine or Midden: The area where droppings are deposited; 'toilet'.
Litter: A group of young animals produced at one birth.

Migrating/migrant: Moving from one region to another, with the seasons.
Nocturnal: Active at night.
Omnivore: An animal that eats both meat and plants.
Pride: A group of three to 20 lions, but may include up to 30 lions.
Rosette: A small group of spots on the leopard's coat.
Scavenger: An animal that feeds on the carcass of an animal it did not kill itself.
Terrestrial: Living on the ground.
Territorial: Staying in a marked-off area, which is defended against others.
Troop: A group of monkeys or baboons.

Photographic Credits

Nigel Dennis: front cover (bottom right), pg1, 3, 4, 6 (IOA), 8, 12, 13, 15, 17, 18 (IOA), 19, 20, 21, 22, 23, 24 (IOA), 25, 26, 29, 30, 31, 32 (IOA), 33, 35, 36, 37, 38, 39, 40, 42 (IOA), 47, 48, 49, 51, 52 (IOA), 55, 56, back cover;
Wendy Dennis: pg5;
R. Haestier: pg53;
Lex Hes: pg28, 50;
Leonard Hoffmann/IOA: pg2, 14;
Peter Pickford: pg41, 43 (IOA), 54 (IOA);
Austin J. Stevens: pg5, 7, 9, 12, 16, 27, 44, 45;
Erhardt Thiel/IOA: pg34;
Lanz van Horsten/IOA: front cover (left, top right), pg46;
John Visser: pg10, 11;
David Thorpe/IOA: pg54 (illustration).

IOA = Images of Africa

Vervet Monkey (page 13)